The Library of Explorers and Exploration

FRANCISCO VÁSQUEZ de CORONADO

Famous Journeys to the American Southwest and Colonial New Mexico

Lesli J. Favor, Ph.D.

the rosen publishing group's
rosen
central

*This book is dedicated to the explorer who
lives in the heart of each of us.*

Published in 2003 by The Rosen Publishing Group, Inc.
29 East 21st Street, New York, NY 10010

Library of Congress Cataloging-in-Publication Data

Favor, Lesli J.
Francisco Vásquez de Coronado : famous journeys to the American
Southwest / Lesli J. Favor.— 1st ed.
    v. cm. — (The library of explorers and exploration)
Includes bibliographical references (p.) and index.
Contents: The age of discovery—The lure of the New World—
The seven cities of Cíbola—Culiacán and beyond—Attack on Cíbola—
Side parties led by captains Tovar, Arellano, and Díaz—A turning
point—Expeditions by captains Tovar, Cárdenas, and Alvarado—
The attack at Tiguex—Destination Quivira—Coronado and the
future of the Spanish empire—Chronology.
ISBN 0-8239-3619-8 (library bdg.)
1. Coronado, Francisco Vásquez de, 1510–1554—Juvenile literature.
2. Explorers—America—Biography—Juvenile literature. 3. Explorers—
Spain—Biography—Juvenile literature. 4. America—Discovery and
exploration—Spanish—Juvenile literature. 5. Southwest, New—
Discovery and exploration—Spanish—Juvenile literature. [1. Coronado,
Francisco Vásquez de, 1510–1554. 2. Explorers. 3. America—
Discovery and exploration—Spanish. 4. Southwest, New—
Discovery and exploration.]
I. Title. II. Series.
E125.V3 F38 2003
979'.01'092—dc21
                                                            2002003206

CONTENTS

Inspired by rumors about the legendary Seven Cities of Gold, Francisco Vásquez de Coronado, along with 300 Spanish soldiers and more than 1,000 Indians, was among the first Europeans to explore the territory later known as the American West.

INTRODUCTION
THE AGE OF DISCOVERY

F rancisco Vásquez de Coronado was one of the first European men to explore the American Southwest. He was a conquistador—a Spanish military leader, who, in the sixteenth century, conquered parts of North America. He followed in the footsteps of other conquistadors before him, such as Francisco Pizarro, who conquered Peru, and Hernán Cortés, who conquered Mexico.

From 1540 to 1542, Coronado led his army from Compostela in New Spain (now Mexico) northward through the present-day states of Arizona, New Mexico, Texas, Oklahoma, and Kansas. Coronado was in search of the fabled Seven Cities of Gold, but he found only a strange new land—a landscape of stone houses and the natives who lived in them. When he returned to Mexico City, his expedition was deemed a failure because he had found no gold or wealth of any kind. Today, however, Coronado is considered one of the foremost European explorers of this great period of discovery. His expedition into the North American interior is worth far more than the elusive gold he sought, for the knowledge he gained became both a legacy of triumph for the Spaniards who eventually colonized the West, and one of tragedy for the Native American tribes who lost their lives and land.

1

THE LURE OF
THE NEW WORLD

. . . at the time Francisco Vásquez was appointed governor, he was traveling through New Spain as an official inspector, and in this way he gained the friendship of many worthy men who afterward went on his expedition with him.
—Pedro de Castañeda, *The Journey of Coronado*

Coronado was born into a noble family in Salamanca, in west-central Spain, probably in the year 1510. His parents, Juan Vásquez de Coronado and Isabel de Lujan, ensured the quality of his education, but as a youth he understood that his older brother would inherit the family wealth according to custom. Coronado would need to seek his own fortune. When Don Antonio de Mendoza, who had been appointed the first viceroy of New Spain, asked him to serve as his personal assistant there, Coronado accepted. He was twenty-five years old. (A viceroy, or vice-king, is the king's personal representative and rules a country on behalf of the king.) In the year 1535, Viceroy Mendoza reported directly to King Charles I of Spain.

Coronado must have been excited to serve the Spanish Crown in the New World. Thanks to the conquistadors, sixteenth-century Spain was the greatest empire at the time and included most of South and Central America.

Coronado had witnessed this gloriously exciting time of world exploration during his youth when Spain sent conquistadors to unmapped regions of the New World. Less than two decades before Coronado was born, Christopher Columbus discovered the land we now call America while searching for a sea route to Asia. His discovery of the Indies, as he believed it to be, captivated the imagination of other adventurous men such as Francisco Pizarro, Ferdinand Magellan, Hernán Cortés, Álvar Núñez Cabeza de Vaca, and Coronado, who led their own expeditions for Spain in the decades that followed.

Coronado would have known some details of how Pizarro discovered Peru during his expedition of 1526–1528. Pizarro conquered the Incas in 1533, claiming the country for Spain. Spaniards were fascinated by the wondrous tale of how Pizarro had captured the emperor of the Incas, Atahuallpa, and obtained gold and silver from him. Coronado had heard, too, of Magellan's famous voyage ending in 1522, the first circumnavigation of the globe.

This is a nineteenth-century illustration of a bridge and cathedral in Salamanca, Spain, the birthplace of Coronado. An explorer born into a noble family in 1510, Coronado had his first government appointment in the New World at the age of twenty-five.

Upon his arrival in New Spain, Cabeza de Vaca faced incredible hardships including starvation, thirst, disease, slavery, and a brutal hurricane in order to explore the New World. He was one of only four survivors of Pánfilo de Narvaez's expedition to the Florida coast in 1528.

Around the same time (1519–1521), Hernán Cortés led an expedition into Mexico, conquering the Aztec Empire for Spain.

Cabeza de Vaca

The conquistador who had the most profound effect on Coronado, however, was Cabeza de Vaca, an explorer who had served as treasurer to a Spanish expedition to Florida in 1528. Although a hurricane shipwrecked the expedition on the coast of present-day Texas, Cabeza de Vaca was among the survivors who were, at first, cared for by natives and later enslaved by them. Eventually, he and three others escaped and slowly made their way to the northern province of New Spain. Upon their arrival in 1536, they told tales of marvelous cities filled with great riches of gold and jewels. Cabeza de Vaca described wondrous cities to the north of New Spain, and the Seven Golden Cities of Cíbola, where Indians lived in large, multi-storied houses. He was certain that these were the fabled Seven Cities of which many a conquistador had dreamed.

Cabeza de Vaca's report of Cíbola helped set the course for the remainder of Coronado's life. Prior to his arrival in New Spain, however, Coronado settled into his role as assistant to the viceroy. Viceroy Mendoza, as the personal representative of King Charles I in the New World, was charged with increasing the revenues of the Spanish Crown and governing the Mexican Indians. Coronado achieved these goals, establishing character traits of being responsible, capable, and friendly.

In 1537, Coronado earned a favorable reputation in Spain when Viceroy Mendoza asked him to quell an African slave revolt. With the aid of Mexican Indian allies, Coronado put down the revolt and restored order. He publicly hanged several of the leaders of the rebellion. Coronado's leadership ability and actions, though they had deadly consequences for the Spanish slave population, pleased the viceroy, who began considering him for a more powerful role.

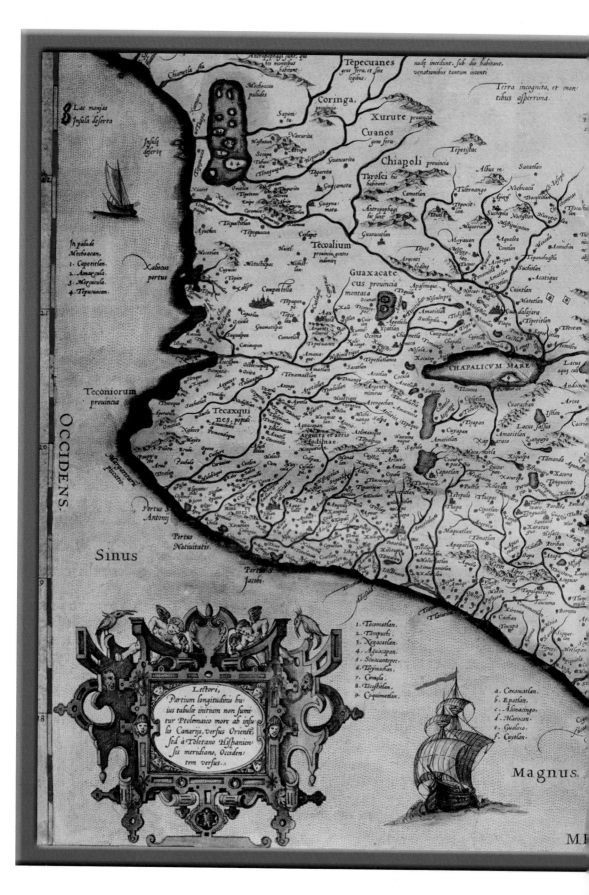

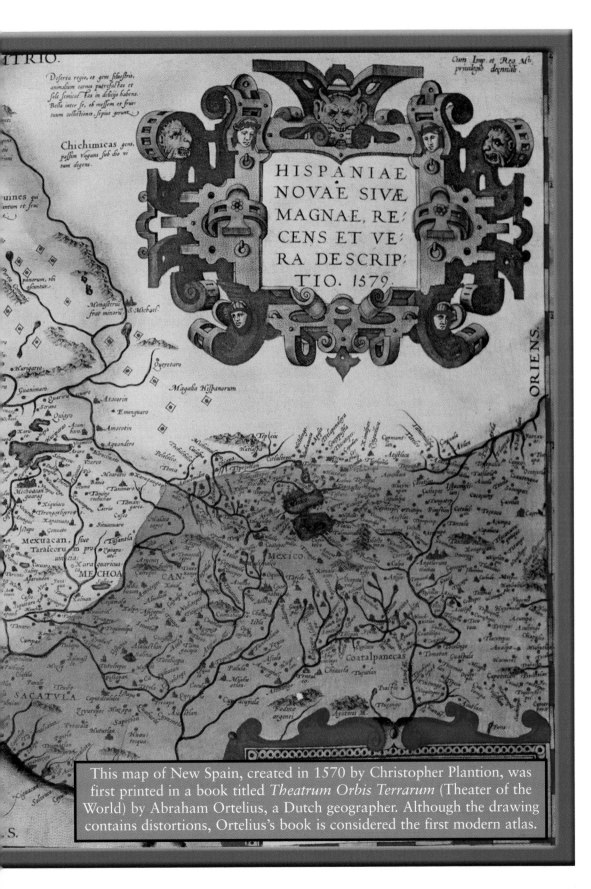

This map of New Spain, created in 1570 by Christopher Plantion, was first printed in a book titled *Theatrum Orbis Terrarum* (Theater of the World) by Abraham Ortelius, a Dutch geographer. Although the drawing contains distortions, Ortelius's book is considered the first modern atlas.

Wealth and Power

Coronado, still an ambitious administrator, not only established a firm footing in the political circles of New Spain, but also socialized with the most respected and wealthy of its families. His marriage to the beautiful heiress Beatriz de Estrada increased his social status, for she belonged to one of Mexico's most powerful Spanish families. Her father, Alonso de Estrada, had been the treasurer of New Spain, and she brought to the marriage a large estate. Some people even rumored that Alonso de Estrada was a son of His Majesty Ferdinand, who ruled Spain from 1479 to 1516. By all accounts, Coronado was happy and loved his wife dearly.

By 1538, Nuño de Guzman, the governor of New Galicia, was put in prison for raiding Indian villages to capture slaves. Soon after, Mendoza made Coronado the governor of this province on the western coast of New Spain. New Galicia consisted of four main cities: Guadalajara, Purificación, Compostela, and Culiacán. Coronado gained power with the promotion, for he was no longer an assistant but a leader. He was twenty-eight years old. Coronado began improving the region by building roads and planning defenses against Indian attacks. He established friendships with prominent men of the region, many of whom he would later rely upon. Soon, however, Coronado's successful political and social life would take a dramatic turn.

2

THE SEVEN CITIES
OF CÍBOLA

I pursued my journey until within sight of Cíbola, which is situated on a plain at the skirt of a round hill. It has the appearance of a very beautiful town, the best that I have seen in these parts . . . Saying to the chiefs who had come with me how beautiful Cíbola appeared to me, they told me that it was the least of the seven cities . . .
——Fray Marcos de Niza, *Narrative of Fray Marcos*

Cabeza de Vaca's bedraggled group of shipwreck survivors had arrived in New Spain in 1536 with riveting tales of riches in the unexplored North. The curiosity created by these tales had only increased over time, for Mexico City was filled with young men, who, swept away by fantasies of fame and fortune, longed to be conquistadors. They had heard of the expeditions of Pizarro and Cortés, which had resulted in great wealth for the explorers. Upon hearing of Cabeza de Vaca's tales, they must surely have imagined how they themselves could be heroes for the Spanish Crown, the next conquistadors to win riches in a new land.

South American Indians panning Gold. Seville 1535

Native Americans' lives changed dramatically during the sixteenth century once Europeans began arriving in the New World. Many found that they were forced to mine their own lands for gold to appease Spanish rulers.

Viceroy Mendoza was also captivated by the stories of the golden cities. In February 1539, he ordered Fray Marcos de Niza (Friar Mark of Nice) and a small party to travel north to determine whether the golden cities existed and, if so, where they were located. Estévan, an African slave who had survived with Cabeza de Vaca, went as his guide.

By the summer of 1539, Fray Marcos returned to New Galicia and submitted reports of his journey to Governor Coronado. On the way, he said, Indians had told him about a large valley where people wore cotton garments and golden ornaments. He said their vessels were made of gold, and that they used flattened gold pieces as sweat scrapers. But the valley lay inland, and to explore it would have been a violation of the viceroy's mandate to remain near the coast. Although Fray Marcos did not enter the valley, his descriptions of it must surely have inspired dreams of riches in anyone who heard his stories. Perhaps there were great rooms full of gold and silver, as Pizarro had acquired in Peru.

Distant Gold

Fray Marcos described the Seven Cities, saying he had seen one beautiful city from a hill some distance away. It was larger than Mexico City, with multi-storied, stone houses. He said he put a small cross on the hill in the name of Viceroy Mendoza, to show that he took possession of the entire province in the name of Spain.

Despite Fray Marcos's proximity to the mystical city, he did not enter it or venture close to its walls. He had recently learned that the Indians in Cíbola had killed Estévan, a man who had gone there several days in advance of Fray Marcos to announce the friar's arrival.

Later, the natives told Coronado that they killed Estévan because they thought he was a spy sent by men who wanted to conquer them. The Indians also found it suspicious that Estévan, who was an African, claimed to come from a country of white men. According to other accounts, Estévan angered the Indians by demanding jewels and women. As a result, they killed him, but allowed most of his traveling companions to go free. These men returned to the main exploration party, where they told Fray Marcos what had happened. According to the friar, he and his

Coronado sought ornate gold pieces like this Mixtec disk. They were made by native people using the *cire perdue* (lost wax) technique.

companions left the province in great haste, fearful that they, too, would be killed. Some historians believe that Fray Marcos never actually traveled within sight of Cíbola, and that he fabricated much of his tale.

Facts and Legends

What is to be made, then, of the tales of gold that Fray Marcos is said to have relayed to the Spanish leaders, or of the promise of riches that lured Coronado on his infamous expedition into the New World? Some degree of legend seems to have developed around the friar's report, even in the months following his return. As the report and Coronado's expedition were recounted throughout time, legend was passed along with fact.

As historian William K. Hartmann explains in a letter to the author, "The 'standard' story about Marcos coming back and officially reporting a city full of gold and jewels seems to be an example of false history handed down generation after generation. His formal report, which we still have, says nothing about gold in Cíbola. What we don't know, though, is how much he might have speculated about gold, in informal conversations.

"Regardless of what he actually said, Fray Marcos became a scapegoat for the expedition's failure, once the soldiers reached Cíbola and found no transportable riches."

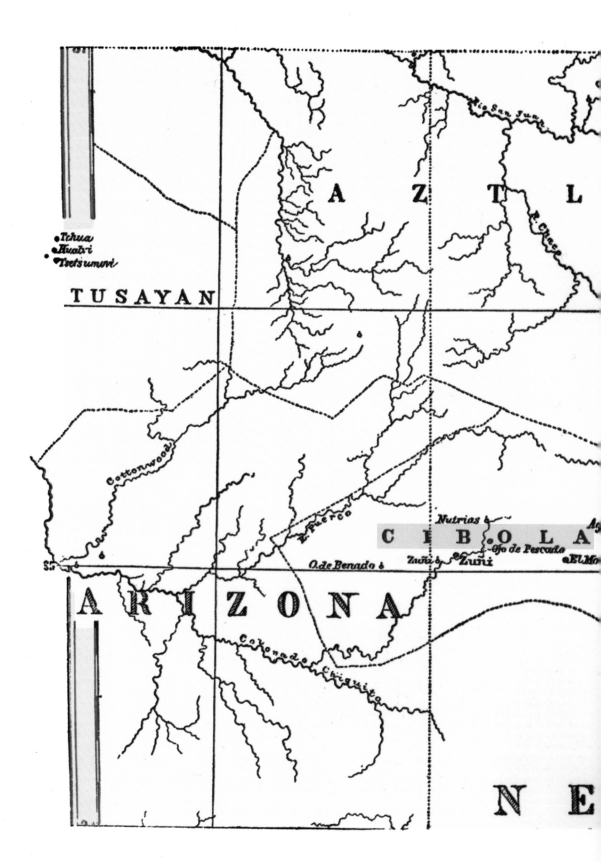

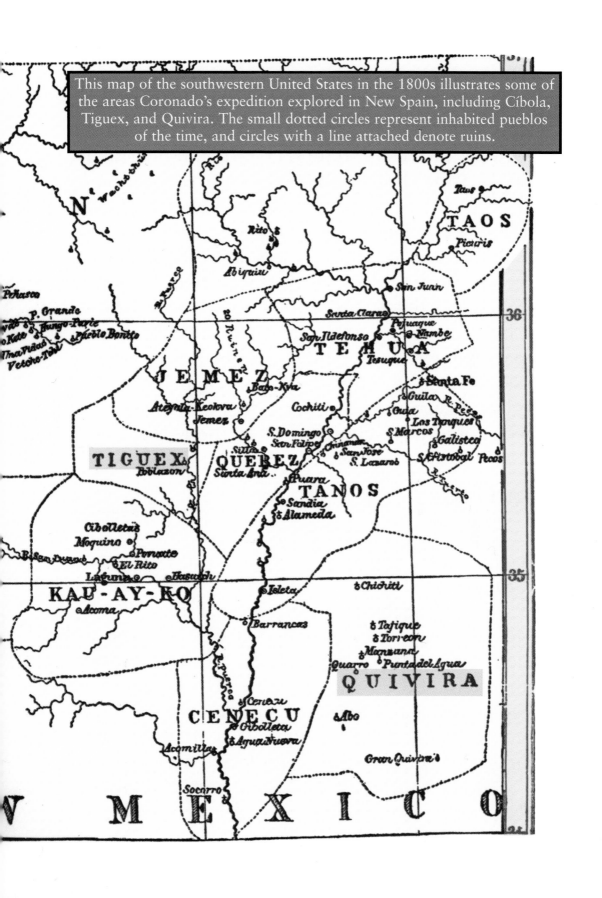

This map of the southwestern United States in the 1800s illustrates some of the areas Coronado's expedition explored in New Spain, including Cíbola, Tiguex, and Quivira. The small dotted circles represent inhabited pueblos of the time, and circles with a line attached denote ruins.

Whether true or not, Fray Marcos's words sparked a chain of events that would take Coronado's army on a three-year hunt through the Southwest and result in much death and heartache. Upon hearing Fray Marcos's report, Coronado traveled to Mexico City to inform Mendoza of the exciting news. Pedro de Castañeda, who chronicled the details of Coronado's entire expedition, described Coronado's rather secretive behavior. "[Coronado] made the things seem more important by not talking about them to anyone except his particular friends, under promise of the greatest secrecy, until after he had reached Mexico [City] and seen Don Antonio de Mendoza." This secrecy could have contributed to the rumors.

The Quest for Cíbola

To organize a properly outfitted expedition to conquer the Seven Cities of Cíbola required a great deal of money and power. Only a few men in the New World had these resources, including Viceroy Mendoza, who immediately raised the money needed to finance the expedition. Wealthy himself, he invested 60,000 ducats. Coronado, who had access to his wife's great wealth, invested 50,000 ducats. Other well-to-do Spaniards supplied large sums of money, too, as did soldiers who invested smaller amounts. Everyone hoped to receive a huge return on their investment when the city's riches were finally attained.

The question now was, who would Viceroy Mendoza name captain-general of the army? Many men would have been thrilled to receive the appointment, but it was Coronado, who had brought Mendoza the news from Fray Marcos, who received this honor. On January 6, 1540, Mendoza named Coronado as head of the expedition. In his chronicle, Castañeda observed that Mendoza chose

Antonio de Mendoza (1490–1552) was the first viceroy of Mexico after the Spanish conquest by Hernán Cortés in 1521.

Coronado "because at this time Francisco Vásquez was his closest friend, and because he considered him to be wise, skillful, and intelligent, besides being a gentleman."

In February 1540, with great fanfare, Coronado's army came together in Compostela. Here, Mendoza would appoint captains and review the troops, charging them with obedience and loyalty to Coronado. Many prominent gentlemen of New Spain eagerly took their places, full of optimism for the expedition to come. Castañeda declared that "they had on this expedition the most brilliant company ever collected in the Indies to go in search of new

Coronado, as portrayed in this detail of a painting by N. C. Wyeth, was respected by his men because he fought along with them. He is best remembered in history, however, as the least inhumane of all the Spanish conquistadors.

lands." (Although the Spaniards knew that the lands they were in were not the Indies, Columbus's name for the inhabitants—Indians, meaning people of the Indies—remained.)

The army included approximately 300 Spaniards and nearly 1,000 Indian allies from central Mexico who had previously joined Cortés to defeat the Aztec Empire in 1521. At least one account recorded the presence of women in the army, wives of some of the Spanish soldiers. To help with the transportation of men and supplies, the army took approximately 1,500 horses and mules and, for food, herds of cattle, sheep, goats, and swine. Fray Marcos, the source of the magnificent stories, would serve as a guide, leading the expedition to the Seven Cities.

In addition, Mendoza sent two ships up the western coast of New Spain under the command of Hernando de Alarcón. Since Fray Marcos reported that the route to the Seven Cities lay along the coast, Mendoza planned to keep Coronado's army supplied from the ships following along in the Gulf of Cortés (the present-day Gulf of California).

As it turned out, Fray Marcos's account of the route was inaccurate, and Coronado's army would never receive the supplies sent for them by ship. For the time being, however, anticipation was in the air, and the army rejoiced in its eagerness to depart.

3

CULIACÁN AND BEYOND

We ought to devote our attention to those Seven Cities and the other provinces about which we had information—that these should be the end of our enterprise. With this resolution and purpose, we all marched cheerfully along a very bad way, where it was impossible to pass without making a new road or repairing the one that was there, which troubled the soldiers not a little, considering that everything which the friar had said was found to be quite the reverse . . .
—Francisco Vásquez de Coronado, in his report to
Viceroy Mendoza, August, 1540

In February 1540, Coronado led his army out of Compostela toward Culiacán, the northernmost Spanish town in New Spain. Just beyond lay the unexplored frontier. Colorful banners snapped in the breeze above the soldiers, whose spirits soared. Adding to the festive mood, Viceroy Mendoza traveled with the army for two days before turning back to resume his duties in Mexico City.

Soon, however, Coronado and his men understood the harsh reality of their journey. Each man was responsible for his own baggage, but because they had little experience as travelers, many of them brought too

Coronado's soldiers most likely wore brigandine armor, unlike the suit of field plate shown on this soldier. Brigandine armor, made from metal and fabric, was crafted in Italy and imported to Spain. Coronado himself most likely wore plate armor, a more expensive and protective metal suit.

many items and had difficulty in securing the loads to their horses. The animals were out of shape, and with the heavy loads and large herds, progress was excruciatingly slow. Soldiers quickly began lightening their loads by giving items they could spare to people they passed. As Castañeda commented in his report, "In the end necessity, which is all powerful, made them skillful, so that one could see many gentlemen become carriers, and anybody who despised this work was not considered a man."

The first fatality came unexpectedly. During the initial leg of the journey, between the cities of Compostela and Culiacán, the army-master, Lope de Samaniego, took several men to obtain food nearby. They were ambushed by Indians, and several soldiers were shot with arrows. Samaniego received an arrow through the eye and died instantly. The army-master's death was a serious loss to the expedition, and the soldiers reacted with confusion. Coronado acted quickly to punish the Indians and hanged several of them from trees.

An Unexpected Welcome

Coronado led his army onward and in April, just before Easter, he reached the outskirts of Culiacán, at the edge of the frontier. The citizens of the town asked that the soldiers not enter until after Easter, and they obliged. As it turned out, the townspeople had prepared a special welcome for their governor and his army.

The day after Easter, the army approached the town. As they did so, the townspeople came out on foot and with horses and appeared as though ready for battle. They maneuvered several bronze pieces of artillery into position and pretended to defend the town. Some of Coronado's soldiers went forward and enacted a skirmish with them, and each side fired its artillery. Then the townspeople fell back to show the town had been "captured." Castañeda said that the entire event "was a pleasant demonstration of welcome, except for the artilleryman who lost a hand by a shot, from having ordered them to fire before he had finished drawing out the ramrod."

The army rested in Culiacán for several days, stocking up on provisions and preparing for the next difficult stage of the journey. Many soldiers took the opportunity to lighten their loads further by giving extra clothing to the families with whom they lodged. In a letter to Viceroy Mendoza, Coronado reported that when they left Culiacán none of them carried any item that weighed more than one pound.

During this time, one of the soldiers decided he would rather not continue on the expedition. The soldier, Truxillo, pretended to receive a vision from the devil. He "reluctantly" allowed himself to be brought before Coronado, where he described the vision. The devil had told him, Truxillo said, that if he killed Coronado he would be able to marry his wife, the lovely

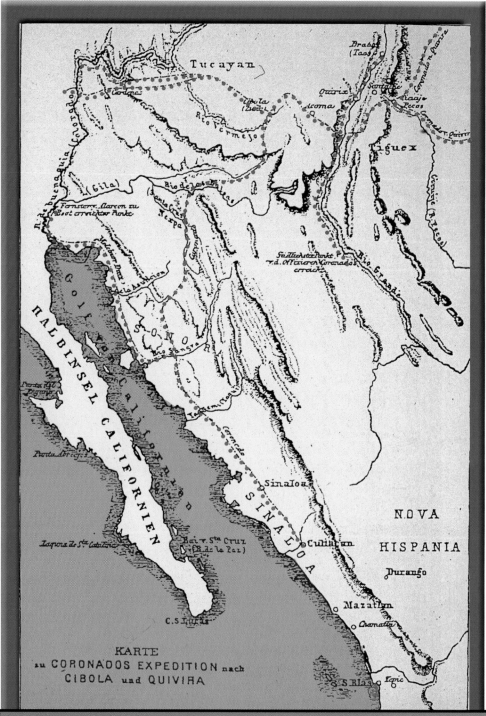

This map, which details Coronado's expedition of 1540–1541, shows his path. He traveled along California's gulf coast from Culiacán and Cíbola to Tiguex and Quivira in search of the legendary Seven Cities of Gold in Nova Hispania (New Spain), now Mexico.

Beatriz, and share her wealth. Upon hearing this, Coronado ordered the soldier to remain in Culiacán. This result, as many agreed, was precisely what Truxillo wanted.

Growing Doubtful

On April 22, 1540, Coronado led his army out of Culiacán. During the first two weeks of travel, he grew increasingly impatient with the expedition's pace. He selected fifty horsemen, a few foot soldiers, and many Indian allies—a group that would be able to travel much faster. Leaving the other soldiers and animals under the charge of Tristán de Lunay Arellano, Coronado set out with his advance party.

Fray Marcos had promised an easy journey through green valleys and open trails, but it had only been rough and dangerous. As a result, the army had to forge a new trail. The friar had also promised only one small hill, but the army found mountain ranges. With determination, Coronado's men hauled their harquebuses (portable guns) up and down hills and mountains and across rivers. The herds of animals fared poorly. The lambs "lost their hoofs" on the rocks and had to be left behind to follow at a slower pace. Most of the corn was lost, and since the army survived on cornbread, food became very scarce.

Accompanied by a Native American guide, Coronado crosses the plains of Kansas on horseback on his expedition to conquer the legendary Seven Cities of Cíbola, in this 1905 painting by Frederic Remington.

Coronado had sent Captain Melchior Diaz and several soldiers to scout ahead and verify what they could of Fray Marcos's report. The small party went as far as Chichilticalli without finding any evidence that what Fray Marcos had reported was true. They returned and reported to Coronado, who tried to keep the disappointing news from his men. Word of the discrepancy soon leaked out, however, and it became even more of an exaggeration. Disturbed and discouraged, the soldiers began to doubt Fray Marcos. The friar hastened to assure them he could indeed lead them to a land where their hands would be filled with wealth. Still, he managed to smooth over their feelings and satisfy their concerns, for the time being at least.

Coronado reminded the army that it was reasonable that part of the journey would prove fruitless. Their true goal was the Seven Cities, not the wilderness that surrounded them. Coronado felt that he had assured his troops, for he wrote privately to the viceroy that, despite the difficulties, the army marched cheerfully.

Near the end of May, Coronado arrived in a valley where he and his army rested. When Cabeza de Vaca had passed through several years earlier, the natives, Lower Pima Indians, had brought him many hearts of animals, so he named the place Corazones (Hearts) or, by some accounts,

Valley of Hearts. By the time Coronado's army arrived in Corazones, many horses had died of starvation. A few Indian allies had also perished. Unfortunately, the valley had no corn for the starving army. Coronado sent Captain Diaz into the nearby Señora Valley to trade goods for food. Finally, the army could replenish and recover.

Unforeseen Dangers

Coronado led the men onward, farther across the present-day boundary between Mexico and Arizona, attempting to remain near the coast where they could eventually reach supply ships. Not far from the Gila River they reached Chichilticalli and the ruins of an earthen house. Once there, however, they realized that they were fifteen days' journey inland from the sea. Coronado recalled that Fray Marcos had said the sea was very close to the route—within sight of it, in fact. The discrepancy between the friar's report and the reality of the route ignited a new storm of doubt, anxiety, and dismay among the soldiers. Swayed by the friar's accounts, the army had expected Chichilticalli to be far grander than what they finally came across: one deserted house made of red earth, without a roof. They must have wondered if anything the friar told them was true.

These ruins, approximately 1,200 small rooms surrounding a courtyard, were once part of the Kuaua Pueblo visited by Coronado in 1540. The site is now part of the Coronado State Monument in Bernalillo, New Mexico.

Coronado allowed the army to rest for only two days because their food was dwindling at an alarming rate. As they pushed onward, they found that there was not even grass for the horses in their first few days of travel. The terrain grew rougher, drier, and more dangerous than before. More horses died from hunger and exhaustion, and some of the desperately hungry soldiers died from eating poisonous herbs. Besides the hardships of hunger and thirst, this dusty, rocky wilderness, studded with cactus, was full of dangerous wildcats, mountain lions, and other animals the Spaniards had never seen before.

At last the army made its way out of the mountainous region and into one where rivers crisscrossed the land. With relief they found grass for the horses, as well as fish, nuts, and mulberries for themselves. By July, Coronado knew they were nearly within sight of Cíbola when they reached a muddy, reddish waterway, which they called the Vermilion River. Shortly after, they encountered the first Indians in this strange land.

4

THE ATTACK AT CÍBOLA

The first fury of the Spaniards could not be resisted, and in less than an hour they entered the village and captured it. They discovered food there, which was the thing they were most in need of.

—Pedro de Castañeda, *The Journey of Coronado*

Army-master Cárdenas, who had reached the Vermilion River in advance of Coronado, met a few natives who promised to feed the hungry soldiers. He gave the Indians a cross and told them they had nothing to fear, for the army came "in the name of His Majesty to defend and help them." Soon Coronado arrived and spoke with some of the Indians, giving them paternosters (words of prayer) and cloaks and telling them not to fear.

Although Spanish soldiers had the horses, steel weapons, and firearms to overwhelm the Native American tribes, the true devastation of the Indians came from the spread of European diseases such as smallpox, measles, typhus, and influenza (flu).

Ambushed

As soon as the Indians left for their village, Coronado commanded Cárdenas to take some men and follow them to see if there were any places in the trail where they might be ambushed the following day. Coronado's wisdom probably saved many lives. Cárdenas found a passage in the trail where an attack could be easily launched, and he camped there to guard it. Later in the night the Indians came to occupy the same pass, and, finding Coronado's men already there, they attacked. The noise of musket fire must have been shocking to these natives, who had never before heard this sound. The Indians sounded a trumpet and retreated, and Cárdenas held the pass.

The sounds of battle and shouts of Indians carried through the night. Back at Coronado's camp, some of the less experienced soldiers were so startled that, according to Castañeda, they put saddles on their horses backward.

That night, Coronado knew that his hopes for gold would soon be realized—or dashed. One thing was certain, however: The natives of Cíbola had killed Estévan in part to protect their province from conquerors. Coronado, a conquistador for Spain, must certainly have thought carefully about the best way for an exhausted, hungry, and weakened army to approach the

Seven Cities. Despite the prospect of an unfriendly reception at Cíbola, General Coronado was convinced that the only way to save his soldiers from starvation was to gain access to food. He later told the viceroy, "I thought we should all die of hunger if we continued to be without provisions for another day."

The First Disappointment

At long last, on July 7, 1540, after nearly six months of exhausting travel, Coronado led his men within sight of the Seven Cities. Populated by Zuni Indians, Cíbola lay in the western area of modern New Mexico. The village directly before Coronado's army was Hawikuh. According to Castañeda, Hawikuh was "a little, crowded village . . . of about 200 warriors . . . with the houses small and having only a few rooms, and without a courtyard." The terraced city was surrounded by flat plains of reddish earth with high mesas rising in the background.

The soldiers, who expected a mystical golden city of houses studded with gemstones, were disappointed. Without doubt, they were angry and blamed Fray Marcos for misleading them about the city's riches. Castañeda wrote that "when they saw the first village . . . such were the curses that some hurled at Friar Marcos that I pray to God He may protect him from them."

The Native American Zuni tribe's Dance of the Great Knife depicted in this painting is just one example of the type of culture seen by Coronado and his men during their sixteenth-century travels.

A Sacred Land

The general had no way of knowing that his army had arrived during a sacred ceremony of the summer solstice. The Spaniards approached from the west, the same direction from which the Zuni were expecting their tribesmen to return from a pilgrimage to a sacred lake. The Zunis were greatly disturbed, for no one was to cross the path of the returning pilgrims. As a result, some of the Zunis tried to intercept the foreign army.

Coronado sent Cárdenas, two priests, and a few men to speak with the Zuni. They announced the standard *requirimiento* that the Spanish recited to the natives of land they claimed. The *requirimiento* commanded the natives to "acknowledge the Catholic Church as the ruler and superior of the whole world, and the high priest called Pope, and in his name the King and Queen" of Spain. The *requirimiento* also informed the Zuni that if they did not agree and submit, the Spanish would declare war on them and make slaves of their women and children.

The Zuni priests were unimpressed with the Spanish *requirimiento*, and one of them made a line in the sand with white cornmeal. The message was, "Do not cross into this area. It is sacred." The Spaniards did not understand. With hunger gnawing at their stomachs, they thought only of obtaining food and would not retreat.

One of the Zunis shot an arrow through Fray Luis's sleeve, and other shots followed. Coronado's men begged him to allow them to fight back, but he hesitated as the viceroy had ordered him not to engage in battle. But the Indians became bolder and moved closer to the soldiers' horses to shoot their arrows. Finally, with approval from the priests, Coronado gave the order to attack, setting in motion the first pitched battle between a European army and natives of the Southwest. Unprepared to face an enemy firing muskets, some of the Indians were killed while others fled to the hills.

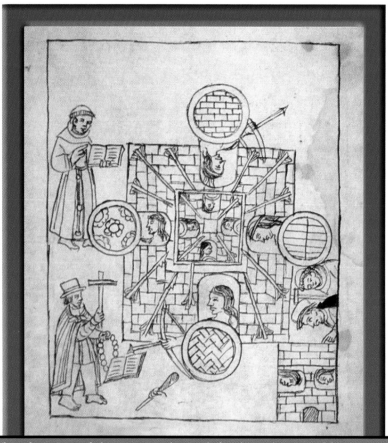

This drawing of the Zuni Indians defending their pueblo against Coronado, made by a Mestizo (half-Spanish and half–Native American) artist, clearly shows that religious beliefs were central to both cultures. This merging of religion became one of the most important points of interaction between the Spanish and the tribes of the Southwest.

Attack

Driven by hunger, Coronado assembled his army for an attack on the city. The soldiers were weak, but to delay meant slowing the possibility of eating. Coronado saw that there were no doors at ground level. To get inside, the Zunis used ladders to reach the rooftops and entered through special holes there. They had retreated within these near-impenetrable walls, pulling the ladders behind them.

Coronado, however, was not halted for long. He ordered his men to charge a ladder he saw leaning against an outside wall. He also commanded his crossbowmen and musketeers to fire their weapons. The starved and exhausted soldiers tried their best. Coronado wrote to the viceroy, "The crossbowmen broke all the strings of their crossbows and the musketeers could do nothing, because they had arrived so weak and feeble that they could scarcely stand on their feet."

The Zunis stood atop the high walls and dropped large stones down upon the heads of the Spanish soldiers. Seeing the bright armor of Coronado, many Zunis aimed their rocks and arrows in his direction. He was struck on the head by a great rock, and would have been seriously injured if not for his "very good headpiece." Coronado's other injuries included an arrow through the foot, two small facial wounds, and bruises on his arms and legs. When the rocks knocked him to the ground again, Cárdenas and Hernando de Alvarado threw themselves atop the general and took the brunt of falling stones, saving him from serious injury.

Despite the condition of the soldiers, they conquered Hawikuh in an hour. Once inside the city, the ravenous Spaniards raided the pantries. For the moment, filling their stomachs with food was more important than filling their purses with treasure. Coronado had found the Seven Golden Cities, but all he had to show for it was corn and beans.

5

THE SECRET PLAN

Captain [Díaz] had the Indian who had confessed the affair killed secretly, and that night he was thrown into the river with a weight, so that the Indians would not suspect that they found out. The next day they noticed that our men suspected them, and so they made an attack, shooting showers of arrows, but when the horses began to catch up with them and the lances wounded them without mercy and the musketeers likewise made good shots, they had to leave the plain and take to the mountain, until not a man of them was to be seen.
—Pedro de Castañeda, The Journey of Coronado

While Coronado and his soldiers rested in Cíbola, other soldiers who had been given particular missions carried on. Before leaving Culiacán in New Galicia, Coronado had commanded Tristán de Lunay Arellano to remain with some soldiers. They would wait for the harvest, gather provisions, and meet with the army later. When Arellano left Culiacán, he followed the route Coronado had taken to the Valley of Hearts. Here, Arellano founded a town and named it San Hieronimo de los Corazones (Saint Jerome of the Hearts).

Soon after embarking on the long trek across the desert, Coronado's soldiers rid themselves of any unnecessary baggage. The animal herds they traveled with slowed their journey so much that the soldiers were often forced to travel separately.

The town served as a gathering place for members of the army who were not with Coronado in Cíbola. By autumn, Melchior Diaz and Juan Gallego arrived in Corazones, too. Coronado had sent Diaz to take command of Corazones while Gallego was sent on a journey back to New Spain with a letter to Viceroy Mendoza. Fray Marcos, much disgraced, accompanied Gallego. Due to the soldiers' intense anger and disappointment over the absence of wealth in Cíbola, it was no longer safe for the friar to stay with the army.

Diaz took command of Corazones, choosing eighty men to remain there. The rest he sent with provisions to meet Coronado's army in Cíbola. Diaz selected another group to go with him in search of the supply ships in the gulf. The weakest men of the army remained at Corazones under the command of Diego de Alcaraz.

Escaping to California

Diaz marched northwest from Corazones for approximately 450 miles (720 km). Nearing the coast, he encountered the Yuma tribe of Indians, whose great size and strength fascinated him. When six Spaniards tried to carry a heavy log to a fire and could not lift it, one of the Yuma easily raised it to the top of his head and carried it alone to the fire. The Yuma lived together in large houses built into pits in the ground with straw roofs. They baked loaves of bread in the hot ashes of their fires and wore no clothing, even in bitterly cold temperatures. When Diaz discovered a large river nearby, he named it Firebrand River (the present-day Colorado River).

Diaz learned that ships had been seen downriver, about fifty miles north of its mouth at the Gulf of California. Hoping to meet Captain Alarcón and the ships there, Diaz found only letters from the captain buried beneath a marked tree. Alarcón had brought the ships as far as he could in search of Coronado's army but had finally returned to New Spain. Alarcón also wrote that California was not an island, as everyone had believed. He had realized this fact when his ships came to the mouth of the Colorado River emptying into the gulf. California, he learned, was a peninsula of the mainland and formed the western side of the gulf.

From there, Diaz led his army up the river looking for a place to cross into California. Some of the Yuma in this region agreed to help him build rafts. As they were assembling the rafts, one of the Spaniards noticed a party of armed Indians crossing the river. The soldiers quietly captured an Indian and then tortured him until he revealed the Indians' plot: They were planning to attack the soldiers when they were divided—some on the opposite bank, some on rafts, and

In the battles in Tiguex, the Spanish burned more than 100 Native Americans at the stake during a winter-long bloodbath in 1540–1541.

some on the first bank. That night, Diaz had the captured Indian killed, weighted down, and thrown into the river so that the other Yuma would not find out that the soldiers knew of their secret plan.

The next day, however, the Indians became aware of the Spaniards' suspicion, and they immediately attacked them with bows and arrows. Diaz's men fought back from horseback with lances and muskets, sending the Indians fleeing into the mountains. After this, Diaz's men crossed the river safely and became the first Spaniards to blaze an overland route from New Spain to California.

Unfortunately, soon after crossing, Diaz was fatally injured. From horseback, he threw a lance at a dog that was chasing his sheep, and the lance stuck upright in the ground. As his horse carried him forward, the butt of the lance accidentally pierced his groin. Diaz died from the injury before he was able to see Coronado again, and his soldiers returned to Corazones.

An Offering of Peace

While Diaz's men were occupied with their trek to the coast and their crossing of the Colorado River, the soldiers who had been sent from Culiacán to Cíbola with supplies for Coronado made their way north.

51

Because Coronado had been largely careful to pass peacefully through the region, these soldiers encountered no trouble from the natives. In a province called Vacapan, natives offered them preserves made from prickly pear cactuses. But after eating the preserves, many of the soldiers fell ill with headaches and fever. The Indians had intended no harm, however, for they did not attack the weakened soldiers. The illness lasted twenty-four hours. As soon as the men were able, they continued their march northward.

They passed Chichilticalli, with its single broken-down, roofless house. Three days later, they examined an amazing item Coronado had left on the trail for them to find. It was a gigantic horn, six feet long and as big around at the base as a man's thigh! The men were awestruck by this strange find. But they soon encountered another fascinating sight: a herd of animals that reminded them of sheep, except that they were huge and had long brown wool and large horns. The soldiers followed the buffalo, but were unable to catch any.

The most dangerous part of the soldiers' journey was its final stretch. When they neared Cíbola they were struck by a tornado, which was closely followed by a heavy snowstorm. These forces of nature chased the men into caves, where they huddled in the bitter cold.

Coronado at various times called the American bison—an animal never before seen by Europeans—a cow or a bull. He and his soldiers found themselves amazed by its wooly fur and oversized horns.

Most of the Indian allies were unused to such icy temperatures. The following day, they were in such intense pain from the cold that they could not walk. They were instead carried on horseback while the Spanish soldiers proceeded on foot. In this manner they reached Cíbola, where General Coronado had food and beds waiting.

This Zuni pueblo is thought to be the pueblo that was known in Coronado's time as Cíbola.

6

A TURNING POINT

It now remains for me to tell about this city and kingdom and province, of which the father provincial [Fray Marcos] gave Your Lordship an account. In brief, I can assure you that in reality he has not told the truth in a single thing that he said, but everything is the reverse of what he said, except the name of the city and the large stone houses.
—Francisco Vásquez de Coronado, in his report to Viceroy Mendoza, 1540

While Coronado was severely disappointed not to find riches in Cíbola, he continued to perform his duties to the viceroy with devotion. He claimed the province for Spain and wrote a report (which would be carried to Mendoza by Gallego) describing the cities. Where the general had expected to find good brick houses decorated with turquoise, he found only stone structures constructed as apartments, three to five stories high, with more rooms underground. The houses were entered by means of ladders, which were movable and allowed access to the roofs.

The Seven Cities of Cíbola, Coronado found, was a cluster of villages known collectively as Cíbola. The village occupied by Coronado, which he named Granada, consisted of about 200 houses. Coronado estimated that approximately 500 families lived in and around this town. He told Viceroy Mendoza about the other villages and made sketches of the region on animal hides.

Coronado speculated that the natives were not intelligent enough to have built these villages. He described how they wore little clothing, which to his mind seemed to indicate primitiveness. He told of their painted murals, one of which he enclosed for Mendoza to see, along with his crude, newly drawn map.

Hidden Treasures

Since the Indians had taken many of their possessions when they fled the village after Coronado's attack, he suspected they were hiding their turquoise from him. Coronado found "two points of emerald and some little broken stones which approach the color of rather poor garnets," and he set these aside for Viceroy Mendoza as well. Later, the soldier in charge of the packet of gems lost them.

Coronado also reported on the animals in the area, listing bears, tigers, lions, porcupines, wild goats, deer, leopards, "sheep as big as horse[s], with very large horns and little tails," and cows (probably bison). He also found fowl, probably turkeys, which he reported tasted better than those in Mexico. The Indians told Coronado that they did not eat these birds, but raised them only for their feathers.

Three days after Coronado captured Hawikuh, some of the Zunis returned and offered gifts of turquoise. After accepting the gifts, Coronado informed them that all the natives of this region must become Christians and serve the king of Spain. The Indians returned to their houses, but apparently only to gather their belongings. The following day they fled back to the hills. Coronado sought a leader from the other villages to spread the word that the Indians should return to their towns and serve the king.

Some of the Indians told Coronado of a prophecy that was spoken fifty years before of men who would come and conquer the whole country. The Indians believed Coronado and his men were those conquerors.

With most of the army coming together in Cíbola, Coronado was faced with a decision. Having accomplished the expedition's goal of finding Cíbola, he could go back to Mexico, but the idea of returning without gold was an unpleasant prospect to him. He was determined to get the gold he had set out to find.

Coronado also had his reputation to consider. Upon setting out on the expedition, he had been favored by the viceroy, and was governor of a large province and son-in-law to an important and wealthy man. Thus far, Coronado's life had unfolded with great success. To return home now would be an admission of failure, an idea he hardly welcomed.

Coronado decided to send scouting parties from Cíbola to investigate other regions. To the west he sent Pedro de Tovar and later García López de Cárdenas. To the east he sent Hernando de Alvarado while he waited at Hawikuh, hoping for news of riches.

7

THIS FOREIGN LANDSCAPE

There were no settlements or farms between one village and another and the people do not leave the villages except to go to their farms, especially at this time, when they had heard that Cíbola had been captured by very fierce people, who travelled on animals which [sic] ate people. This information was generally believed by those who had never seen horses . . .
—Pedro de Castañeda, *The Journey of Coronado*

On General Coronado's orders, Pedro de Tovar took seventeen horsemen, a few foot soldiers, and friar Juan de Padilla, and headed east in search of Tusayán (a present-day Hopi Indian province in Arizona). Zunis living in Cíbola had told Coronado about this province. As Tovar's party approached the area, they encountered no people. They were able to creep up to the edge of a Hopi village without being detected, and there they sat in the darkness and listened.

This Hopi man, photographed by an unknown photographer in 1904, is a descendant of the tribes that Coronado and his men encountered during their sixteenth-century expeditions.

The next morning, however, Tovar's men were discovered. With bows, arrows, shields, and wooden clubs, the Hopi arranged themselves before their intruders. They held this orderly formation while Tovar's interpreter attempted to persuade them to become Christians and loyal subjects of the Spanish king.

In response, the Hopi drew a line in the sand that the Spaniards were not supposed to cross. According to Castañeda, some of the soldiers, who were probably just joking, acted as though they would cross the line. One of the Hopi responded by striking a horse on the side of its head with a wooden club.

Exasperated, Fray Juan said to Captain Tovar, "To tell the truth, I do not know why we came here." Upon hearing the holy man's comment, the soldiers gave the call for battle, "Santiago!" (Saint James), and charged the Hopi. The Indians fled to their village and immediately began emerging with gifts of peace. They offered cotton cloth, animal skins, cornmeal, pine nuts, corn, and birds. Tovar found that these villages were governed in much the same way as Cíbola—that is, by a group of the oldest men. These elders told Tovar about a river to the west where very large Indians dwelled.

Expedition of Captain Cárdenas

Tovar returned to Cíbola with a report for Coronado, who was intrigued by the information about the river and Indians farther west. He ordered another exploring party, this one to be led by García López de Cárdenas.

Captain Cárdenas led his men along the route Tovar had followed to Tusayán. The natives there received them peacefully and helped them stock provisions. The Hopi told them it would take more than twenty days of walking to reach the river to the west.

According to Castañeda, Cárdenas's party was well paced, for in twenty days they reached a deep canyon, at the bottom of which flowed a great river. They were in the high plateau region of northwestern Arizona. The mighty river cutting right through the gorge was the Colorado, and Cárdenas's men were standing on the rim of the Grand Canyon.

The Spaniards had never seen anything like this vast gorge, for the Grand Canyon is up to eighteen miles wide. Nearly 300 miles long, it reaches colorful depths of over a mile with rocky hues of reds and browns.

Besides being awestruck by the grandiosity of the canyon, the thirsty Spaniards, weary from weeks in the dry desert, were tormented by the sight of the unreachable water. For three days, they attempted to find a route down to the river.

This Foreign Landscape

Besides being struck by its sheer beauty, Don García López de Cárdenas and his party—the first Europeans to see the wonderous landscape of the Grand Canyon—were enticed by the opportunity to drink from the Colorado River. However, his expedition spent three days attempting to reach the bottom of the Grand Canyon in 1540, but could not.

From their high vista, the river seemed narrow. Three men attempted to climb down the canyon, but made it only about a third of the way before returning. They reported that the river looked a great deal wider from below and that boulders they had thought were a man's height were actually as high as the "great tower of Seville."

Since the men could not reach the current of the Colorado, each evening they traveled inland from the canyon to find water, returning with a fresh supply. The Hopi guides cautioned that if they walked more than four days farther into the desert there would be no water at all. When the Hopi traveled through the desert, they were much faster than the Spaniards and brought women whose job it was to carry water in gourds. Along the way, the women buried the gourds so that they would have plenty to drink on their return journey.

As Cárdenas stood high above the banks of the Colorado River, he did not know that Captain Melchior Diaz had reached the same waterway farther downstream and had named it the Firebrand River. Unable to go down the Grand Canyon, Cárdenas and his men turned back. On their return trek they came upon a waterfall from which crystals of salt hung. They gathered a supply of salt and carried it back to Cíbola, where they shared it.

Cárdenas gave his report to Coronado, not knowing he had been the first white man to see the Grand Canyon.

The Expedition of Alvarado

During the time Tovar and Cárdenas were exploring west of Cíbola, a group of Indians from the east arrived. They were from Cicúye, and among them was a young man whom the Spaniards nicknamed "Whiskers" because he wore a distinctive mustache. Whiskers and his group had come to offer friendship to the Spaniards and brought them gifts of tanned hides, shields, and headpieces. Coronado accepted the gifts and in return gave them glass dishes, pearls, and bells—items that the Indians had never seen before.

Whiskers told Coronado about giant animals that roamed the plains to the east. One of the men in Whiskers' party had a picture of the animal drawn on his skin, and when the Spaniards saw it they called it a cow. They marveled at the wooly, curly hair on the skin of the animal, not knowing that these "cows" were actually American bison. Coronado gave orders for Hernando de Alvarado to take a group of twenty soldiers and go along with Whiskers to see the huge animals.

In five days' time Alavarado's group reached the rock of Acoma, a lofty sandstone butte in current west-central New Mexico. Here, raiding Indians, much feared in the region, lived atop the rock 350 feet above the surrounding plain. Alvarado found that only a very good musket could shoot a ball as high as the village. To reach it, the natives climbed a stairway of about 300 steps and then climbed the sheer rock face using hand- and toeholds. If enemies attempted to climb up, the Indians had a good supply of large rocks they could drop down on their heads. Atop the rock they were able to raise corn and collect water from rain and snow for survival. The village was virtually impregnable.

When these Indians saw Alvarado's party below, they came down and drew lines in the sand that the Spaniards were not to cross. They appeared ready to fight. However, when Alvarado's men showed that they, too, were ready to fight, the Indians offered peace instead. To show their intent, they rubbed their hands in the sweat of the horses ridden by the Spaniards and then rubbed the sweat on themselves. They made the sign of the cross with their fingers, and they linked arms to show they were united in their offer of peace. Finally, they gave gifts of turkeys, bread, deerskins, pine nuts, corn meal, and corn to Alvarado's men. Alvarado departed peacefully with these provisions.

Tiguex

After traveling three more days, they reached a new province where they were greeted peacefully. Named Tiguex, the province was situated on a wide river, today called the Rio Grande. Alvarado observed that the area was well suited to camp, and he sent word to Coronado to bring the army from Cíbola to winter there. As it was September, Alvarado had plenty of time to explore the land eastward before the coldest season began.

Alvarado soon came to Whiskers' village of Cicúye. For several days there was great festivity and music. Alvarado's men were given gifts of cloth and turquoise. During this time, Alvarado met an Indian slave who wore a headdress that reminded him of the turbans worn by people in Turkey. They nicknamed the slave "the Turk." Captain Whiskers said that the Turk would guide them in their search for the cows.

As Alvarado and his men began looking for the cows, or bison, the Turk told stories that gold and silver could be found in his homeland, Quivira. Alvarado became so excited about the new tales of riches that he decided to quit searching for bison and to report the news of riches to Coronado instead. Upon returning from Cicúye to Cíbola, he found Cárdenas and a portion of the army already in Tiguex, setting up camp. He stopped there to wait for Coronado.

This mural of a figure with lightning and rain is on the wall of a kiva in
Kuaua Pueblo, near Tiguex. A kiva is an underground ceremonial chamber
found in the American Indian villages of the southwestern United States. Most
kivas have murals depicting sacred figures or scenes from the daily life of the
tribe. The murals are painted on adobe plaster with warm,
colorful pigments made from the rich mineral deposits of the area.

8

THE ATTACK AT TIGUEX

As he [Cárdenas] had been ordered by the general [Coronado] not to take them alive, but to make an example of them so that the other natives would fear the Spaniards, he ordered 200 stakes to be prepared at once to burn them alive. Nobody told him about the peace that had been granted them . . .
—Pedro de Castañeda, *The Journey of Coronado*

At Cíbola, General Coronado prepared to take his army to Tiguex on the Rio Grande River, near present-day Albuquerque, New Mexico. Cárdenas and Alvarado's men were already settling there for the winter. Before Coronado left, soldiers under the leadership of Tristán de Lunay Arellano arrived in Cíbola, having come from Señora. Coronado commanded them to rest at Cíbola for several weeks before marching to Tiguex to join the rest of the army.

Coronado had heard about a province of eight villages that he wanted to see, so he decided to investigate them en route to Tiguex. He selected thirty men and, along with guides, set out. They were forced to travel for three days without water. If the season had not been cold, they likely would have been forced to turn back or risk dying of dehydration. Finally, on the third afternoon, they located snow-covered mountains and were able to drink the melted ice. Moving on, they reached Tutahaco, where Coronado heard about other towns down the river. Coronado instead took his men up the river's banks, visiting any villages they passed until they reached Tiguex. Once there, they joined the army.

Stories of Quivira

The Turk was soon brought before Coronado, who listened with interest to his account of the gold that abounded in his homeland. The Turk described how lushly beautiful the land was. The river was two leagues wide (about 6.2 miles or 10 km), and the fish were as big as horses. People traveled in huge canoes with sails powered by forty rowers, and their lords sat on decks shaded by awnings. A golden eagle graced the prow (front) of the canoe. The lord of the country, the Turk said, took naps under a huge tree where tiny bells had been strung, the music of which lulled him to sleep. Everyone ate from silver plates and golden bowls.

Coronado, in order to test the Turk's wisdom, showed him an assortment of metals and asked him if any were, in fact, pure gold. In turn, the Turk convinced Coronado that he knew what gold was when he correctly said that he did not care for any of the metals since they were not. In addition, the Turk claimed that the people in Cicúye had robbed him of his golden bracelets when they enslaved him. Straightaway, Coronado sent Alvarado to Cicúye to demand the Turk's golden bracelets. When Alvarado made the demand, the people of Cicúye told him that the Turk was a liar. They denied the existence of any golden bracelets and his tales that Quivira was a land of gold and silver.

Alavarado then made a decision that the entire expedition would regret. He asked Whiskers and a chieftain of Cicúye to come to his tent, and when they did he put them in chains and took them back to Tiguex. When the Indians at Tiguex saw Whiskers and the chieftain in chains, they were very angry. According to Castañeda, "This began the want [lack] of confidence in the word of the Spaniards whenever there was talk of peace from this time on, as will be seen by what happened afterward." The Turk, however, had achieved some degree of revenge against the people who had enslaved him by causing their leaders to be taken prisoner. The Turk plotted another fate for Coronado and his army.

Assault from Above

Conflict soon developed between the Spaniards and the Indians at Tiguex. Coronado and his army were unprepared for the freezing temperatures of winter, and they did not have provisions of food. They demanded shelter, warmer clothing, and food from the Indians. Many Indians were forced to take off their own cloaks and give them to the soldiers. Coronado's men also drove the Indians from their homes and took their belongings for themselves. One Spanish soldier attacked an Indian woman.

The assault on the woman was the last straw for the Indians. They demanded the soldier be punished, but disagreement arose over which Spaniard was guilty. In retaliation for the attack and general mistreatment by the Spaniards, the Indians killed a soldier who was guarding the army's horses and, as a result, drove the animals off. Some of the horses were collected again, but many were lost.

The following day, Coronado sent Cárdenas to the villages where the Indians were staying to speak with them. He and his men found the villages barricaded, and inside they heard the sound of the Spaniards' horses being chased and shot with arrows. At this, the Spaniards were ready to fight.

Coronado ordered Cárdenas to surround one of the Indian villages and attack it. They chose to ambush the area where the attack on the woman had been reported from. The Spaniards climbed up to the upper stories of the houses and assaulted the Indians from above with crossbows and muskets. Outside the village, more Spaniards and Indian allies broke into the cellars of shelters and filled them with smoke until all the Indians had fled.

Burned Alive

Finally, the Indians begged for peace by making the sign of a cross. Two captains who were on the roofs answered by making the same sign. The Indians, understanding that the Spaniards had agreed to a peaceful resolution, surrendered themselves and were taken to Cárdenas. A great massacre was about to unfold, however.

Cárdenas claimed that he did not know the Indians had asked for peace. Instead, the captain believed they had been conquered. Moreover, he said that Coronado had given him orders that no Indian was to remain alive. His intention was to dominate all the Indians in other villages.

Cárdenas ordered that the Indians be burned alive. When the first group were at the stake, the rest of the captives could hear their anguished

Although the Indians at Tiguex surrendered to the Spanish and begged for mercy, Cárdenas ordered that the Indians be burned alive. A heated battle followed as the native people of Tiguex resisted the brutal conflict.

cries and smell their burning flesh. They realized what was happening and desperately fought back with whatever weapons they could find, including the stakes they were to be burned upon. Those who ran were chased down on horseback and cut down. Every Indian that could be found was brutally killed. Castañeda later wrote that a few may have hidden in the village and escaped later, spreading warnings that the Spaniards did not keep their word when making peace.

Ultimately, Coronado was responsible for the actions of his officers. It is interesting to note that the faithful chronicler Castañeda did not record any punishment of Cárdenas by Coronado for the captain's terrible act against the natives, simply because Coronado probably did condone the attack.

After the bloodshed, heavy snow began to blanket the land. The few remaining natives made no attempt to remain in the village taken over by the Spanish, but gave it up to the conquerors. During the winter months, Spanish soldiers traveled through the snow from village to village, and urged the Indians to make peace. With good reason the natives distrusted the soldiers, and numerous skirmishes erupted as each side attempted to outwit the other. The Spaniards killed hundreds of Indians and captured many villages. Fleeing Indians even attempted to cross the icy Rio Grande River, but many drowned. Others reached the opposite banks only to freeze to death later. In the newly captured villages, women and children were made prisoners and slaves.

The Spanish siege of the villages at Tiguex lasted the winter, ending in March of 1542. Oddly, Castañeda found it surprising that the natives did not return to their villages when the Spanish promised peace, writing, "The twelve villages of Tiguex, however, were not repopulated at all during the time the army was there, in spite of every promise of security that could possibly be given to them."

9

DESTINATION QUIVIRA

I traveled five days more as the guides wished to lead me, until I reached some plains, with no more landmarks than as if we had been swallowed up in the sea, where they strayed about, because there was not a stone, nor a bit of rising ground, nor a tree, nor a shrub, nor anything to go by . . .
—Francisco Vásquez de Coronado, *Report to the King of Spain*

On April 23, 1541, Coronado led his entire army out of Tiguex. They and their herds of sheep and cattle traveled eastward, at last on their way to Quivira. The general's hopes of finding treasure were high, and he was certain the expedition would improve.

When they came to Cicúye, Coronado released Captain Whiskers, who had been his prisoner all winter. He had released the chieftain a few months earlier during the siege. According to some

After first discovering the Missouri River, Coronado erected a cross by its banks with an inscription that read, "This far came General Francisco Vázquez de Coronado," as is depicted in this illustration.

accounts, at this time the Turk met secretly with some men in Cicúye to devise a plan of revenge on the Spaniards. Captain Whiskers presented Coronado with two additional slaves to help guide the army to Quivira, one named Xabe and the other named Sopete. According to the secret plan, the Turk and Xabe would lead the Spaniards out into the desert to die while telling them they were on the way to beautiful Quivira. Sopete, who was tattooed with circles around his eyes, exclaimed that Quivira was not a rich province, but no one believed him.

Unaware of the plan of revenge, the optimistic Coronado marched his army across the Cicúye River (now the Pecos River) and then across western New Mexico toward the modern-day Texas Panhandle. The Turk's story of plentiful wealth must have seemed doubly appealing to Coronado, who had been sent in search of riches but had found only bits of turquoise. He would rather return to Mexico City with bags of gold for the Spanish Crown than arrive poor, ragged, and without any treasure. He surely believed that Quivira would provide the wealth he needed to salvage his reputation.

The army's trek across the flat, featureless plains of New Mexico and Texas was beset by obstacles. Finding little water to sustain the soldiers and horses, Coronado reported that his thirsty army "often had to drink it so poor that it was more mud than water." The vast plains were so devoid of landmarks that men who left the group to hunt often found themselves lost. The tramp of hundreds of soldiers' feet left no marks on the prairie grass, which quickly sprang up after being flattened. One soldier who ventured too far from the camp was never heard from again. When Coronado sent a scouting party ahead, the men left piles of rocks and buffalo dung to mark their trail.

The Querechos

On the plains, the army encountered huge herds of the buffalo they called cows. Not a day passed when they did not see the strange animals. After seventeen days of marching, Coronado's army came across a nomadic tribe of Indians, the Querechos, who traveled with buffalo herds and relied on them for nearly every aspect of their lives. The Querechos ate raw buffalo meat, drank the animals' blood, dressed in buffalo skins, and slept in hide tents. They loaded their belongings on the backs of dogs each day, which they used as pack animals. Castañeda wrote, "[W]hen the load gets disarranged, the dogs howl, calling someone to fix them right." Coronado asked the Querechos if they knew anything of Quivira, but they did not.

One day the army was resting in a ravine when a horrific hailstorm hit. Huge chunks of ice hurtled down upon them from the sky. Panicking in the storm the horses attempted to flee, but they were halted by the boundaries of the ravine, and most were injured. The icy missiles from the sky ruined tents and left great dents in the metal of the soldiers' helmets. Hailstones smashed all the crockery, making the collection and transport of water and food even more difficult.

Still relying on the Turk's guidance, Coronado instructed his army to continue forward. He could not know that the Turk was deliberately leading them away from Quivira, hoping that they would die or that he would find a chance to escape. However, the grassy plains were good pastureland for the animals and the soldiers learned to hunt from horseback.

The Teyas

While soldiers were hunting buffalo in the area of what is now called the Palo Duro Canyon in Texas, they encountered hunters from another nomadic tribe. The Spaniards called them the "Teyas," mistaking their greeting of "teyas," or "friends," for the tribal name. (The state of Texas was named from this tribal word.) According to Coronado, the Teyas were large people, as the Querechos were, and had painted faces and bodies.

When Coronado asked the Teyas about Quivira, they told him that the land was not rich, as the Turk had claimed. Quivira was a poor province with houses made of straw and animal hides, and there was only a very small supply of corn to eat.

Coronado was disturbed by this news and remembered how he had before followed rumors of riches only to be disappointed. Moreover, the Teyas insisted that the trail to Quivira lay to the northeast, not to the east where the Turk was guiding them.

Coronado questioned the Turk and the other two guides again. The Turk admitted he had lied about the size of the houses in Quivira. However, he insisted that his tale of its riches was truthful. Since the Teyas and Sopete disagreed strongly with the Turk over this matter, Coronado was thrown into a quandary. Whom should he believe?

While deciding what to do, Coronado studied the landscape and the condition of his army. The men had gone for many days eating only buffalo meat because their corn was gone. Water was very scarce and, according to the Teyas, Quivira lay at a distance of forty days' journey.

Rather than risk the lives of his men unnecessarily, Coronado decided to send most of his soldiers back to Tiguex, where they could recover. He placed Tristán de Lunay Arellano in command of them, while he took thirty horsemen to find Quivira and decide whether the province warranted further exploration.

The soldiers were strongly opposed to returning to Tiguex, for they were still convinced that riches lay waiting in Quivira. Some of them feared that the small group who arrived first with Coronado would claim the treasure for themselves. They desperately wanted to reach this mythical region. Even after Coronado sent his army back, they traveled several days before sending a messenger to ask if the general would let them return to the mission. But Coronado was firm in his decision.

Onward to Quivira

For forty-two days, Coronado and the thirty horsemen traveled across the plains and prairies of Texas, Oklahoma, and Kansas. They survived on buffalo meat cooked over fires of animal dung. Several horses died. They went many days without water.

After crossing into Kansas, they encountered a small band of Indians. Although they were near Quivira, these Indians showed no signs of wealth. Coronado again questioned the Turk and, at last, the truth was revealed. Almost everything the Turk had told the Spaniards was a lie.

At first, the Turk had invented tales of fabulous riches at Quivira so that the Spaniards would take him away from the people of Cicúye, who had enslaved him. Then, to escape the Spaniards, the Turk had planned to lead the army into the desert hoping they would die of hunger. However, the soldiers had learned how to survive on buffalo meat. Still, the Turk had not found an opportunity to escape. Coronado was not alone in the disappointment he suffered, it seemed.

Still determined to see Quivira, Coronado led his army across the final stretch to the province. He found that Quivira was indeed poor, its straw houses not nearly as impressive as those at Tiguex. Some villages cultivated beans and Quivira grew corn.

The Indians, probably ancestors of the Wichita, wore tanned animal skins, not cotton, and ate raw buffalo meat. Coronado deemed them "barbarous," but he still performed his duty to the viceroy and king by claiming the region for Spain and swearing its natives to loyalty to the Spanish Crown.

Coronado's party was well received by the Wichita because Sopete was also from this region. Coronado found nearly twenty-five villages here, with the people from each speaking a different language. The diversity of language was a barrier to Coronado's research, for he wanted to know if there was anything in the surrounding region that warranted a return trip with his army. He sent captains in various directions to find what they could. Eventually, Coronado learned there was nothing in the region besides the simple villages at Quivira. Disappointment must have weighed heavily on his heart.

Coronado also learned that the Turk had not ceased his venomous plotting against the Spaniards. While in Quivira, he had attempted to convince the Wichita, who were allies of his native Pawnee tribe, to attack and kill the soldiers. Although the plan had not worked, Coronado realized the danger in leaving the Turk alive. In response to his latest effort, Coronado ordered his execution. That very night, several soldiers bound the Turk, placed a rope around his neck, and strangled him to death. Coronado's hopes of finding gold in Quivira were over.

10

THE FUTURE OF THE SPANISH EMPIRE

Had he [Coronado] paid more attention and regard to the position in which he was placed and the charge over which he was placed, and less to the estates he left behind in New Spain, or, at least more to the honor he had and might secure from having such gentlemen under his command, things would not have turned out as they did . . . [H]e did not know how to keep his position nor the government that he held.
—Pedro de Castañeda, *The Journey of Coronado*

Coronado noted positive aspects of Quivira and reported them to the king. The land was rich, fertile, and fit for farming. There were plenty of streams and rivers. In the area grew nuts, grapes, and mulberries. In fact, the entire area reminded Coronado of Spain.

After twenty-five days at Quivira, Coronado began the return march to Tiguex in August 1541, arriving at the pueblos on the Rio Grande River by early October. The cold

This detail of a map of the United States shows the variety of harsh terrain and different cultures Coronado encountered as he made his way through what is now known as the American Southwest.

winter would soon be upon them, but this season would be worse than the last since none of the Indians trusted the Spaniards, nor would they supply them with food, blankets, or clothing. Coronado's glorious expedition to find gold in the northern frontier had finally ended on a brittle note of failure.

Nearly Silenced

To make matters worse, Coronado received a serious injury in a riding accident. On December 27, 1541, he was racing with one of his captains on horseback. Suddenly the cinch holding his saddle snapped in two, probably weakened from rot. Coronado was flung to the ground in the path of pounding hooves. He was kicked in the head and nearly killed.

The mighty conquistador lay near death for several days. When he finally began to recover, his progress was slow. Coronado was no longer the ambitious and tireless leader he had once been. During his long recovery, he pondered a prophecy about his future that had been told to him as a young man. As the tale went, Coronado would become a powerful man in distant lands, but he would have a great fall from which he would never recover. Coronado became worried that he would die in Tiguex without seeing his wife and children again.

Despite his promises to the soldiers that they would return to Quivira in the spring to search again for gold, he decided that they should all return to Mexico. The expedition was over. While some wanted to return to New Spain, many others did not. Later, while examining the dismal end to the grand expedition, Castañeda judged the army "unfortunate in having a captain who left in New Spain estates and a pretty wife, a noble and excellent lady, which were not the least cause for what happened." He believed that Coronado's desire to see his wife influenced his decision to end the expedition.

Throughout the winter of 1541–1542, Coronado remained weak. He was unable to ride among his soldiers and encourage them as he once had. His physical weakness, combined with his decision to return, caused many soldiers to lose confidence in him as a leader. The great conquistador, who according to Castañeda "had been beloved and obeyed by his captains and soldiers," now faced their disrespect and disobedience. Soldiers ignored his orders, grumbling about their desire to remain in this strange land to find its riches.

Perhaps worse than the soldiers' change of attitude was Coronado's loss of respect from his religious leaders. Three of these men announced that they would not return to Mexico. Instead, they would stay as missionaries to the natives in this country. Historians have been unable to trace what happened to two of the missionaries, but the fate of Fray Juan de Padilla is known. Indians shot arrows into his head, threw him into a pit, and covered him with rocks. The other two missionaries watched, horrified, but could not save him.

The Long Walk Home

With winter over and the land passable again, Coronado assembled his army. They left the region of the Rio Grande River in April 1542. Coronado, still weak, traveled much of the way on a stretcher pulled by two mules. The soldiers had to guard against Indians, who intimidated them with bloodcurdling yells and poisonous arrows. Just a scratch from one of the arrows resulted in a wound that festered and stank as rotting flesh fell from the bone. At night, the Indians neared the camp and stabbed the Spaniards' horses.

The demoralized soldiers marched along in tattered rags, their hair infested with lice. They had to face the same hardships of hunger, thirst, and physical danger as before, but this time they did not have the fire of hope burning in their bellies to lend them energy and strength. To many soldiers, the prospect of returning as failures was so disturbing that they deserted the army and instead chose to live in small towns they passed in the area of current northern Mexico. Many horses also died from exhaustion and hunger in addition to the dozens lost in battles against the natives. At one point, a soldier who attempted to cross a river was consumed by an alligator in full sight of the army. They were not able to save him.

When Coronado at last led his army into Mexico City that autumn, the soldiers numbered less than one hundred. Viceroy Mendoza was extremely displeased to hear Coronado's report, and he branded the expedition a failure. Coronado's reputation was ruined. Still, he seemed to have recovered enough status to serve the city council in Mexico City.

Coronado, in an effort to restore his reputation, continued to serve the Spanish Crown. With Mendoza's approval, he resumed his post as governor of New Galicia, holding the position for more than two years.

Afterwards, a *residencia*, or official inquiry, convened to look into Coronado's actions as leader of the expedition and as governor of New Galicia. *Residencias* were standard practice. At the inquiry, some of the men that had gone on Coronado's expedition accused him of cruelty to the Indians, poor management, and theft of Indian property. In addition, Coronado was indicted on charges relating to his governorship. As a result, his title was revoked and he was fined. He also lost a number of Indians from his estate. However, in February 1546, a Mexican *audiencia* found him innocent of all charges relating to the expedition.

Francisco Vásquez de Coronado spent the rest of his years living in a grand mansion in Mexico City, raising his son and four daughters and serving on the Council of Mexico City. He had mended his friendship with Viceroy Mendoza and gave his loyal support to the viceroy's policies. The brave explorer died on September 22, 1554, at the age of forty-four, and was buried in Santo Domingo Church in Mexico City.

Coronado had been sent to find wealth, preferably gold and precious jewels like those found in other areas of Spain's growing empire. When he returned from his expedition empty-handed, however, no one had immediately thought to consider the value of the lands he had offered to Spain. Everyone was focused instead on the loss of investment capital and the disappointment that the "Indies" did not contain the opulent riches they expected.

But Coronado had pushed the boundaries of New Spain's frontier farther northward. In the decades following his expedition, the Spanish empire grew to include the central and southwestern United States, upper and lower California, and territory to the east, along the Gulf of Mexico to Florida.

This crossbow bolt head was among the artifacts discovered at the Coronado campsite at Blanco Canyon, Texas, in 1996.

Coronado's trek through the Southwest helped future explorers realize that this land held vast reaches of territory. This included Juan Rodriguez Cabrillo, who explored California's coast by sea, and Juan de Oñate, who in 1598 began a conquest of the Pueblo Indians in New Mexico. Although the Pueblos revolted against the Spanish in 1680, they were brought back under their control in 1694.

Spain established settlements in Texas in 1716 and began occupying upper California in 1769. Over the next century, as Britain, France, China, and Russia claimed territory in the New World, Spain fought to retain control of the territory it had claimed. Boundaries were drawn and redrawn. Treaties were written, battles were fought, and land purchases were made. Finally, the Treaty of Córdoba, signed August 24, 1821, officially ended New Spain's dependence on Spain. Although the territory that Coronado had claimed for New Spain ultimately became part of the United States, he had opened up the New Land and introduced it to the world. Coronado also introduced Christianity to the Southwest by leaving behind missionaries to spread teachings of the Catholic Church.

The maps that he made of the routes, landscape, and rivers of the New World did not survive, and historians are still trying to identify the army's trail. Information in Coronado's reports helped identify landmarks such as the Rio Grande River, the Colorado River, the Grand Canyon, and the pueblos of the Zuni, the Pecos, and the Hopi. Clearly, the soldiers traversed territory in Arizona, New Mexico, Texas, Oklahoma, Kansas, and California, and spread European disease such as influenza and smallpox to the shrinking Indian population.

Artifacts from Coronado's camps are occasionally dug up, throwing new light on the Coronado Trail. In April 1996, a team of archaeologists working in Blanco Canyon, east of Lubbock, Texas, uncovered copper crossbow bolt points and other items most likely left by Coronado's army. As scholars continue to discover points on Coronado's path through the United States, it is as though the conquistadors march once again through the land, if only in spirit.

CHRONOLOGY

1510 Probable year of Coronado's birth.

1535 Coronado goes to New Spain as personal assistant to Viceroy Mendoza.

1536 Cabeza de Vaca's party arrives in New Spain (Mexico) with tales of the Seven Golden Cities.

1538 Coronado takes the post of governor of New Galicia, New Spain.

February 1540 Coronado's army sets out on an expedition to find the Seven Cities of Gold.

July 7, 1540 Coronado's army conquers the Zuni at Cíbola in present-day New Mexico.

Summer 1540 Coronado orders side expeditions into present-day Arizona and New Mexico. Mendoza sends supply ships up the Gulf of California, but they do not reach the army.

Winter 1540 Diaz's side party reaches the Colorado River and crosses into California.

Winter 1540 Coronado's army gathers in Tiguex on the Rio Grande River. Conflicts escalate into a bloody attack during which more than 100 natives are burned at the stake. The siege lasts all winter, until March 1541.

April 1541 Coronado leads his army in search of Quivira, marching through eastern New Mexico, the Texas Panhandle, and Kansas. He sends most of the army back in summer 1541, taking a small party all the way to Quivira. They find no gold.

December 1541 At Tiguex for the winter, Coronado is seriously injured in a riding accident.

April 1542 Coronado leads his army out of Tiguex and returns to Mexico. The expedition is branded a failure because Coronado did not find gold or riches.

1544 An official inquiry into Coronado's conduct as leader of the expedition and as governor brings indictments on several charges. Two years later, he is cleared of all charges relating to the expedition.

September 22, 1554 Coronado dies in Mexico City and is buried there.

GLOSSARY

adobe Sun-dried blocks or bricks of mud, used to build houses in the American Southwest.

audiencia A royal governing body in the Spanish colonies.

Cíbola A province in present-day New Mexico near the Arizona boundary where Coronado found and conquered a group of Zuni pueblos, including Hawikuh. The Spaniards had hoped the Seven Cities of Cíbola would turn out to be the legendary Seven Cities of Gold, but this was not the case. Historians state that Cíbola consisted of six, not seven, pueblos.

conquistador Spanish military leaders who conquered Mexico, Peru, and other parts of America in the sixteenth century.

Culiacán The northernmost village of New Spain, located 300 miles from of the nearest Spanish settlement. Part of the province of New Galicia.

expedition   An exploratory journey whose purpose is to study the landscape and people of a new region and perhaps conquer those people and claim the territory.

Fray   The Spanish word for friar, used as a title with the friar's name, as in Fray Marcos de Niza.

friar   A member of a Catholic religious order.

harquebus   A type of gun that can be moved around. It rests on a support during firing.

Hawikuh   One of the Zuni pueblos in Cíbola. Coronado conquered Hawikuh on July 7, 1540.

Hopi   Native Americans living in pueblos in Arizona. Tovar and Cárdenas discovered the Hopi province of Tusayán during their side expeditions.

Indian allies   Native Mexican Indians who helped Cortés defeat the Aztec Empire and lived peacefully with the Spanish colonists.

mesa   A small tablelike portion of land with a high, flat top and steep sides.

New Galicia   A province in New Spain (modern-day Mexico). The major villages in New Galicia were named Guadalajara, Purificación, Compostela, and Culiacán.

New Land A term for the unexplored territory surrounding Cíbola, used by Pedro de Castañeda in his chronicle of Coronado's expedition.

New Spain Land in the New World under Spanish control, including present-day Mexico.

New World A term used by Europeans to refer to the continents of North and South America.

plains Flat, level land.

province A region of a country, distinguished from other provinces for political or geographical purposes. New Galicia was a province of New Spain. Cíbola was a Hopi province in New Mexico.

pueblo Spanish word for town. A Native American village in the southwestern United States, consisting of flat-roofed communal houses built of stone or adobe.

Pueblos Native Americans who lived in pueblos in the southwestern United States.

Quivira A province in present-day Kansas where Coronado expected to find great riches.

residencia   An official inquiry into the conduct of a public official in New Spain.

siege   A method of conquest whereby a military force surrounds a fortified enemy post and cuts off its supplies, forcing the enemy to surrender.

skirmish   A brief fight or battle.

Santiago!   Literally, "Saint James!" A Spanish battle cry.

Seven Cities of Gold   Cities full of riches, described in Spanish legends.

Tiguex   A Pueblo province on the Rio Grande River near present-day Albuquerque, New Mexico.

Tusayán   A Hopi Indian province in present-day Arizona. Hopis from Tusayán guided Cárdenas's men to the Grand Canyon.

viceroy   A royally appointed ruler of a colony in the Spanish Empire.

FOR MORE INFORMATION

In the United States

Arizona Historical Society
949 East Second Street
Tucson, AZ 85719
(520) 628-5774
Web site: http://w3.arizona.edu/~azhist/general.htm

California Historical Society
678 Mission Street
San Francisco, CA 94105
(415) 357-1848
Web site: http://www.californiahistoricalsociety.org

Institute of Texan Cultures
801 South Bowie Street
San Antonio, TX 78205-3296
(210) 458-2300
Web site: http://www.texancultures.utsa.edu/
    public/index.htm

Kansas State Historical Society
6425 SW Sixth Avenue
Topeka, KS 66615-1099
(785) 272-8681
Web site: http://www.kshs.org

University of Texas at Austin
Texas State Historical Association
1 University Station, DO 901
Austin, TX 78712
(512) 471-1525
Web site: http://www.tsha.utexas.edu

Western History Association
1080 Mesa Vista Hall
University of New Mexico
Albuquerque, NM 87131-1181
(505) 277-5234
Web site: http://www.unm.edu/~wha

In Canada

Indian and Northern Affairs Canada
Terrasses de la Chaudière
10 Wellington, North Tower
Hull, Quebec
Ottawa, ON K1A 0H4
(819) 997-0811
Web site: http://www.ainc-inac.gc.ca/index_e.html

Web Sites

Because of the changing nature of Internet links, the Rosen Publishing Group, Inc., has developed an online list of Web sites related to the subject of this book. This site is updated regularly. Please use this link to access the list:

http://www.rosenlinks.com/lee/frvc/

FOR FURTHER READING

Bolton, Herbert E. *Coronado, Knight of Pueblos and Plains*. Albuquerque, NM: University of New Mexico Press, 1990.

Crisfield, Deborah. *The Travels of Francisco de Coronado (Explorers and Exploration)*. Austin, TX: Raintree Steck-Vaughn, 2001.

Jacobs, William Jay. *Coronado: Dreamer in Golden Armor*. New York: Franklin Watts, 1994.

Marcovitz, Hal. *Francisco Coronado and the Exploration of the American Southwest*. (Explorers of New Worlds). Broomall, PA: Chelsea House Publishers, 2000.

Saari, Peggy. *Colonial America Biographies. Vol. 1: A–L*. Julie Carnagie, ed. Detroit, MI: The Gale Group, UXL, 2000.

Saari, Peggy. *Colonial America Primary Sources*. Julie Carnagie, ed. Detroit, MI: The Gale Group, UXL, 2000.

Stein, R. Conrad. *Francisco de Coronado: Explorer of the American Southwest*. Chicago, IL: Children's Press, 1992.

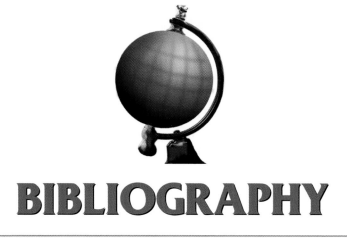

BIBLIOGRAPHY

Crisfield, Deborah. *The Travels of Francisco de Coronado* (Explorers and Exploration). Austin, TX: Raintree Steck-Vaughn, 2001.

Day, A. Grove. *Coronado and the Discovery of the Southwest*. New York: Meredith Press, 1967.

Encyclopædia Britannica Online. "Acoma." Retrieved November 16, 2001 (http://members.eb. com/bol/topic?eu=3595&sctn=1).

Encyclopædia Britannica Online. "Cabrillo, Juan Rodríguez." Retrieved November 5, 2001 (http://members.eb.com/bol/topic?eu=18754&sctn=1).

Encyclopædia Britannica Online. "Cíbola, Seven Golden Cities of." Retrieved August 18, 2001 (http://members.eb.com/bol/topic?eu=84785&sctn=1).

Encyclopædia Britannica Online. "Coronado, Francisco Vázquez de." Retrieved August 18, 2001 (http://members.eb.com/bol/topic?eu=26802&sctn=1).

Encyclopædia Britannica Online. "Cortés, Hernán, Marqués Del Valle De Oaxaca." Retrieved November 5, 2001 (http://members.eb.com/bol/topic?eu=26861&sctn=1).

Encyclopædia Britannica Online. "Grand Canyon." Retrieved August 18, 2001 (http://members.eb.com/bol/topic?eu=38422&sctn=1).

Encyclopædia Britannica Online. "Magellan, Ferdinand." Retrieved November 5, 2001 (http://members.eb.com/bol/topic?eu=51193&sctn).

Encyclopædia Britannica Online. "Mendoza, Antonio de." Retrieved November 5, 2001 (http://members.eb.com/bol/topic?eu=53297&sctn=1).

Encyclopædia Britannica Online. "Mexico, History of." Retrieved November 5, 2001 (http://members.eb.com/bol/topic?eu=115537&sctn=1).

Encyclopædia Britannica Online. "New Spain, Viceroyalty of." Retrieved November 5, 2001 (http://members.eb.com/bol/topic?eu=56901&sctn=1).

Encyclopædia Britannica Online. "Núñez Cabeza de Vaca, Álvar." Retrieved November 5, 2001 (http://members.eb.com/bol/topic?eu=57924&sctn=1).

Encyclopædia Britannica Online. "Pacific Mountain System: Study and Exploration." Retrieved November 5, 2001 http://members.eb.com/bol/topic?eu=119998&sctn=11).

Encyclopædia Britannica Online. "Pizarro, Francisco." Retrieved November 5, 2001 (http://members.eb.com/bol/topic?eu=61785&sctn=1).

Encyclopædia Britannica Online. "Spain, History of," Retrieved November 5, 2001 (http://members.eb.com/bol/topic?eu=115203&sctn=1).

Encyclopædia Britannica Online. "Vespucci, Amerigo." Retrieved November 5, 2001 (http://www.brittanica.com/eb/article?eu=77157&tocid=0&query=amerigo%20vespucci).

Engels, Andre. Discoverers Web. "Francisco Vásquez de Coronado." Retrieved September 5, 2001 (http://www.win.tue.nl/cs/fm/engels/discovery/coronado.html).

Garst, Shannon. *Three Conquistadors: Cortés, Coronado, Pizarro.* New York: Julian Messner, 1947.

Hallenbeck, Cleve. *The Journey of Fray Marcos de Niza.* Dallas, TX: University Press in Dallas, 1949.

Hartmann, William K. Planetary Science Institute. "Coronado's Exploration in the American Southwest." Retrieved September 9, 2001 (http://www.psi.edu/hartmann/coronado/coronado.html).

Jacobs, William Jay. *Coronado: Dreamer in Golden Armor.* New York: Franklin Watts, 1994.

Jensen, Malcolm C. *Francisco Coronado.* New York: Franklin Watts, 1974.

Knoop, Faith Y. *A World Explorer: Francisco Coronado.* Champaign, IL: Garrard Publishing Co., 1967.

Ladd, Edmund J. "Zuni Pueblo." *Encyclopedia of North American Indians.* Frederick E. Hoxie, ed. Boston, MA: Houghton Mifflin, 1996.

Miller, Jay. "Pueblo, Rio Grande." *Encyclopedia of North American Indians*. Frederick E. Hoxie, ed. Boston, MA: Houghton Mifflin, 1996.

PBS Online: New Perspectives on the West. "Francisco Vázquez de Coronado (1510–1554)." Retrieved August 18, 2001. (http://www.pbs.org/weta/thewest/people/a_c/coronado.htm).

PBS Online: New Perspectives on the West. "The Journey of Coronado." Retrieved August 18, 2001 (http://www.pbs.org/weta/thewest/resources/archives/one/corona1.htm).

PBS Online: New Perspectives on The West. "Report to the King of Spain." Retrieved August 18, 2001 (http://www.pbs.org/weta/thewest/resources/archives/one/corona9.htm).

PBS Online. New Perspectives on the West. "Report to Viceroy Mendoza." Retrieved August 18, 2001 (http://www.pbs.org/weta/thewest/resources/archives/one/corona8.htm).

"The People." Vol. 1 of 9 in *The West,* directed by Steven Ives and produced by Ken Burns. The West Film Project, Inc. PBS videocassette: 1992, 82 min.

Saari, Peggy. *Colonial America Primary Source*s. Detroit, MI: The Gale Group, UXL, 2000.

INDEX

About the Author

As a young girl, Lesli J. Favor lived for several years in central Mexico, east of where Coronado led his army out of Culiacán. She has visited each of the states in the Southwest where the conquistador guided his expedition. She is married to fellow Texan Steve Favor and lives in Dallas, a few hundred miles from Coronado's route through the Panhandle. She received her Ph.D. from the University of North Texas and was assistant professor of English at Sul Ross State University Rio Grande College. She currently writes books and educational materials for young people.

Photo Credits

Series Design

Tahara Hasan

Layout

Les Kanturek

Editor

Joann Jovinelly